Hello, I'm here.

The true stories of Nottingham's prostitutes.

The 'Hello, I'm Here' Project,

POW and Platform 51.

Published November 2013

ISBN:978-0-9927532-0-7

Cover Photography: Nick Clague

POW
16 Independent Street
Radford
Nottingham
NG7 3LN
www.pow-advice.co.uk
Phone. 0115 9249992

Contents

About the author

The 'Hello, I'm Here' Project

The Hello, I'm Here project aims to address the needs of girls marginalized by society for their involvement in prostitution. Working closely with the charity POW our project strives to provide these women with the opportunities and inspiration that will enable them to achieve what we firmly believe they deserve. Our vision is the removal of all preconceptions, stereotypes and prejudices to allow these women to consider a life without prostitution and a future they can embrace with confidence.

POW

POW promotes health and dignity in prostitution through empowerment, support and peer education for people involved in the sex industry.   POW works with anyone involved in, affected by or at risk of becoming involved in prostitution. POW's clients are chaotic and vulnerable with complex needs, which often go hand in hand with drug addiction and alcohol misuse. Secondary issues of homelessness, mental health, domestic and sexual violence are common.

POW delivers a holistic service which is individually assessed and dependent on clients needs; providing a free, comprehensive, confidential, full-time drop-in and outreach service to those affected by prostitution and drug misuse; providing information, support, advocacy; other agencies referrals; counseling & advice on matters relating to - personal safety whilst working as a prostitute; sexual health screening; drug prevention and intervention work; social support; contraception service. Allowing the client to make informed lifestyle changes whilst developing routes out of prostitution.

Platform 51

Platform 51 is a national charity that supports girls and women to take control of their lives.

In Nottingham they run an outreach project offering personal development, training, support, therapeutic groups and counselling to girls and women.

Platform 51 have been working in partnership with POW for a number of years to deliver creative therapeutic group work to service users. 'Hello, I'm here' was born out of an opportunity identified in those groups. Platform 51 project and arts workers Angela Warren and Rebecca McNish delivered a series of creative writing and artistic groups to gather stories and artwork for this book to share the stories of the women and men accessing POW.

'Bonnie and Clyde'

My mum was a heroin user and she died a heroin user when I was 14.

I came home from school and I found her dead, with a needle in her arm, she was a sort-of pale blue colour. I had a hard childhood. From the age of 7 and upwards strange men used to come round, they'd pay my mum to abuse me. Some were gentle and bought me football kits, a kind of father figure, others were into drugs and child abuse. When I found her dead, I was sad but mostly relieved, I could go and live with my Nan.

When I was 17 I became really angry. My first drinking session ended up in me having my stomach pumped, I went with a boy shortly after, I didn't like it. I knew I was gay even then.

By the time I was 18/19 I was a DJ in a pub and experimenting with cocaine. When my Nan died, she left £20,000, a huge amount of money and I began to throw wild parties and spend money on staying in hotel rooms. I got involved with my ex-girlfriend Hannah, who was a crack user. The money started to run low and I became an escort, for women, mainly businesswomen or lawyers. I'd charge about £200-300 an hour, they'd take me to Paris or Greece, fancy dinners, many just wanted company, not all of them wanted sex. I put a deposit down on a house and became manager of a pub, I was still escorting here and there.

Hannah didn't like it, so I stopped, she was jealous of me being with other women. I got into crack, it made me aggressive and soon I was spending £200 every other day.

Hannah began to come back home with loads of money, her neck covered in love bites; I began to wonder what she was doing. I followed her one night, she was having a threesome with two

Asians in a car-park. I smashed their windows in and dragged her home.

Then I started to go on the beat, I was the "new" girl, the favourite. By then I was rattling, I needed something to come down off the coke, something to chill me out. I tried heroin. I'd never wanted to, not after mum but I was craving a new buzz.

Heroin is nicer than sex, it's the best feeling in the world- it made me horny for 2 weeks! I couldn't inject it myself, only Hannah could do it for me.

I ended up in prison, Hannah was supposed to take care of me but she didn't. She spent my money and let my flat get taken over my "yardies" or Jamaican drug-dealers. She was raped and stopped prostituting. When I got out, I was so embarrassed and ashamed. I really wanted my flat to be there waiting for me, to help me stay clean.

Hannah looked like Dot Cotton, the drugs had aged her massively. I kicked the shit out of her. I had to look after us both and feed both our habits, I turned to sleeping with men again, most of the time giving head with condoms on. Hannah and I did some "shows" for a couple of clients, but I'd never let them have sex with her. We got another flat, but she began sleeping with loads of men.

Pretty soon, working the street wasn't enough, there were new girls out there now, the new favourites. I had to try and find another way. I began to steal drugs. I'd watch where the Jamaican's would hide them in Kinder Eggs in graveyards and then dig them up and take them. I once found £1700 worth of Cocaine and about £400-£500 of heroin.

Then things began to change, this German guy was going around giving girls about £400 a night to let him beat them with chains. Hannah began to consider it. I even did at my most desperate point.

The police were patrolling the beat more and more, handing out ASBO's making it hard to work. The German guy found Hannah, I don't know where I was, I feel bad I wasn't there. After she spent the night with him, she couldn't lie on a bed for 2 weeks. He was kind, giving her food and wine and then when the money was on the table he turned into a monster. She had strangulation marks and her back was beaten black and blue. He wanted blood.

I realised we needed money, I became a "grass." The police paid me to go into brothels and crack-houses and find out when the big drop would be coming in, big names, powerful people. I had a secret phone and everything, I even signed a contract to say I wouldn't tell anyone, but I did, I told Hannah. From then on I was shit scared she'd tell someone and I'd end up dead. It started to become obvious, even though the police would also attack me when they made a raid.

Once I was in a crack den, (the house of some nonce of paedophile who was terrified of the Jamaicans) and the police busted in. The Jamaicans threw the drugs on the floor, they tried to deny they were theirs. I got taken to the station and let out the back door, they shook my hand and gave me more money. I stopped informing because I was scared about being found out. I was worried about Hannah telling someone too.

I burgled a house. I was so desperate. I was out of my mind and left my DNA behind on a cup in the kitchen. In court when I found out it was an old ladies house, a lady in her 90's, I felt worthless. I tried to take my life in prison. I was so ashamed and the police hated me. They felt like I'd stabbed them in the back. They beat me when they arrested me. I got 18 months and did half. I deserved it.

When I came out, the Jamaicans were looking for me; they knew I'd been stealing the drugs from the Kinder Eggs. Two prostitutes invited me to the graveyard to score, I went and before I knew anything, a plastic bag was put over my head from behind and I was bundled in the back of a car.

I was held in a house with about 10 Black and Jamaican men for 11 days. They took Hannah too; they'd rape us in front of the other, urinate on me and set my hair on fire. They slashed my face with a samurai sword and struck my skull with a crowbar. I now have Epilepsy because of it.

It was humiliating but you just shut yourself off. I thought I was going to die. One day, I heard a care-taker round the back of the house, moments later I heard sirens. I'd been raped for days and I couldn't walk. Black men are big. I didn't want to prosecute, I was worried about my family and my sisters received a death threat. I felt like I deserved what had happened, what I did to the old lady and having beaten up Hannah I felt like I was worthless.

I spent some time in a safe house. I wanted to go home but the police said no. I began importing drugs, in peanut butter jars from Jamaica and did time for that. I've been in 3 different rehabs and have now been more or less drug free for a year and a half. I want to become a councillor for other users.

I'm still so angry at my mum, I was born a user; she was an addict and gave birth to me in Holloway prison. I don 't know how my mum got into drugs, men probably. My grandparents were very well respected people. I still don't know if Hannah has told my secret, that I was a "grass."

I think she's still using. She has 3 kids now.

I can't see her anymore and won't, we're like Bonnie and Clyde.

'Working Girl '

Its £10 for a hand job, £20 for Oral, £30 for straight sex, £50 for sex and oral. I don't do anal, but some girls do.

We don't call ourselves prostitutes – I describe myself as a Working Girl. The official term for us at the moment is "sex workers".

Some punters are actually quite nice and become regulars. Some punters are dodgy and we have photos or descriptions of them at our support groups.

You would be amazed at some of the things the punters want us to do for them. There was one bloke who just wanted to take my shoes off. That's all, no sex. He paid me £150 for that. I told him he could keep the shoes because they had only cost me a tenner. Another bloke wanted me to take my shoes off, run around the garden to get my feet dirty and then let his dog lick them clean!

A few years ago, this old man drove me to Calverton Pit. He told me to get out of the car and started to slap me about. I was so scared, I thought I wouldn't be going home that night because he was going to kill me. But then he just stopped and gave me £80. I said to him, "What's this for?"

He replied, "£10 a slap". So I said,

"Do you want to do it again?"

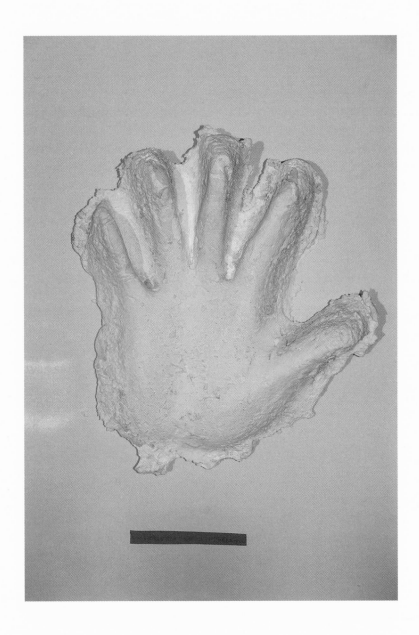

'We'll live with it forever'

I'd find a guy and my man would be waiting to rob him- It's called clipping.

I got into it through a habit of crack and heroin when I was 29. I just couldn't stop robbing.

This guy picked me up and I saw a Sony Ericsson on the side and thought I'm having that. I even robbed the dealers. I made more from stealing than prostituting.

I know some girls who will do stuff for a tenner. It's dangerous out there. They're lucky to be alive. You just learn to survive and run.

I started cannabis when I was 11 but I don't think that's what starts it. Some people take weed and are perfectly fine. You don't realize it at the time but when something like heroin catches you, you're so vulnerable. It takes hold of you.

Junkies are clever people, geniuses really, they think up all sorts of new ways to make money. We used to put water into vodka bottles and gravy into Bailey's bottles and then sell them.

My kids were perfectly aware of what was going on. My son knew me before it all started and after it, he rebelled and went off the rails. His education was ruined. My background definitely affected me.

It's shit for the kids. Both me, my mum, my dad and my son have gone to prison.

Getting out of this situation was the hardest thing I ever had to do. I struggled to go into rehab because of my children. It's really difficult being separated from them. I was still a robber too though so it was really hard.

I put crack cocaine use down to mental problems. Not to be scared of that stuff is crazy. I was one of the lucky ones because I was only using for 5 years.

It's much harder to do with kids. I had to put all that back together. I'm a lucky one because I still have my kids. Seeing the effect it had on them gave me my strength to carry on and that's why I do what I do now.

Social services are no good. There are some good ones but there are no support packages. I think there's got to be an alternative treatment plan within the community.

My determination is definitely not to let my sons be affected by it. My daughter is now an A* student. You can definitely change it around. I think it's more secluded though because of the shit you're smoking.

I don't know what I would've done without my mum. She was always there when I needed her.

Running's not an option you just need some serious hard work and determination. I remember when I was starting to go to interviews and handing over CV's with 6 pages of criminal convictions, but you've got to keep trying. My partner and I always say we'll live with it forever.

To my beautiful children.

'Not our Game'

Poem: Not our game

This is the rhyme I thought I'd write,
For all my colleagues who work by night,
For all the girls who stand and wait,
For the punter that will buy their mate.

To all of you who don't know this game,
Don't drive around and shout out names,
Cause we ain't no different than your sister or mother,
Except for the fact we've been paid by your brother.

So we sell our bodies to gain some wealth,
And we go to the clinic to check our health,
We have our laughs, our ups and downs,

But we're only out to get some pounds.

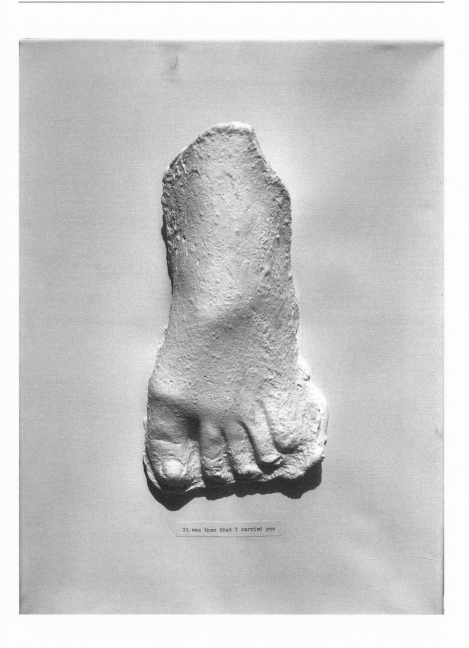

'I'm keeping my baby'

I knew people that were using drugs and ended up in prostitution.

The worst was my friend.

Her boyfriend was hooked on drugs and her baby was taken into care. I used to look after it for her.

I was raped when I was 9, I realised then that other girls were exaggerating about penis sizes'.

I was a fairly violent child, but the home was too quick to call the police when I was naughty. They didn't realise the situation I was in and they make the same mistakes now.

When I got pregnant I ended all ties with anyone who was a user or a street-worker because I wanted to keep my baby.

To my beautiful, little monkey.

'Sarah'

I've been threatened with beatings by a client who demanded their money back. Once I came close to being raped.

I've pulled a friend out of a car as a man started to punch her and seen countless women with bruised and bloodied faces. Never once did I show concern, outwardly at least, because on the streets you cannot show fear.

One guy threatened that if I didn't give him his money back he would punch me. You are supposed to take your money first, but he said he wanted extra and wouldn't go to the bank.

Being raped and attacked is quite common if you're a sex worker. I've seen girls out there on crutches, with broken arms. I wouldn't go back after that. If someone had broken my arm it would take me time to get my courage up and go back out there. It makes you scared when you see people that have been beaten up.

You can't go out on the street and have the fear factor, you have to put on something that you are not. I've never been raped but I've been close to it. When I worked in Norwich a guy was going round in a van. When he picked me up I noticed there was blood on him. He paid me and he started to get violent, I just kept talking until I could get out of there. I have been selling sex for 20 years and I've seen violence increase on the streets.

I've travelled to Leicester, Derby, Norwich, Ipswich and Aberdeen because working on the Forest Road beat might mean my teenage son and the rest of my family could see me. It is a danger out there at the moment. There are a lot of men that you agree a price with and then they want to barter and they don't want to pay you. It's them that are doing the attacking and raping.

Me and my mate were working out there once and the guy had dropped me off by the lights. I heard something and thought that it sounded like my friend. I ran across the road to the car and he was punching her. He said she had robbed him but she hadn't. I could have had that punter.

These days there are too many men out there that are taking working girls for granted. They are there to have their own way. There are so many girls being attacked. Girls are being robbed by non-customers, they watch them get in and out of cars and then attack them because they know they have cash.

At the age of 15, I remember cowering behind bins in Leicester, waiting for a car to pull up. I told myself I was selling sex because I loved my boyfriend. He had suggested I earn some money as a prostitute to help pay for his drug habit and help him buy nice things.

I became addicted to drugs and was out on the street every day and night, desperate to get enough cash to pay for my next hit. I loved the guy I was with. I decided to do it to help him out. He suggested it. I hated it. He used to take me to Leicester and I used to stand behind the bins when I saw a car.

I don't know if it was fear of the client or worrying that someone would recognize me. With my first ever punter I didn't feel scared, I felt like I was in control, but as soon as it was done I felt dirty. I couldn't scrub myself hard enough but I just carried on.

I got on crack and heroin while I was with him. Twenty years on and with two children, I have been clean for a month and have not worked on the streets for seven months. I now work from my phone, arranging to meet clients, using a number I share with a friend. I have robbed people, shoplifted and spent time in prison. I kept returning to prostitution to feed my drug habit.

I desperately wanted to stop. I started taking drugs in 1998. The first ever drug I took was speed, then weed, then crack and then heroin, this was what got me most addicted. With heroin it's a physical addiction. Your body needs it, you feel physically ill without it. You get stomach cramps, leg cramps, twitching. You are always chasing that first ever time you took it.

Nothing matters. The only thing on your mind is crack and heroin. Eating, sleeping, bathing, don't matter, it's just exchanged for drugs, drugs, drugs. I was out there every night and day to make enough money for drugs. Back when I first started, a lot of the girls on the beat were out there for their man, it wasn't about drugs. Now most of the girls are on class A drugs and doing it to support their habit. I know a few people that have died through drug overdoses.

I wanted to stop it all. I wanted to be back to normal. There's more to life than putting myself in danger. It may happen to me one day, I'm not invincible. I might be the one that ends up in the gutter today.

Then who's going to look after my kids?

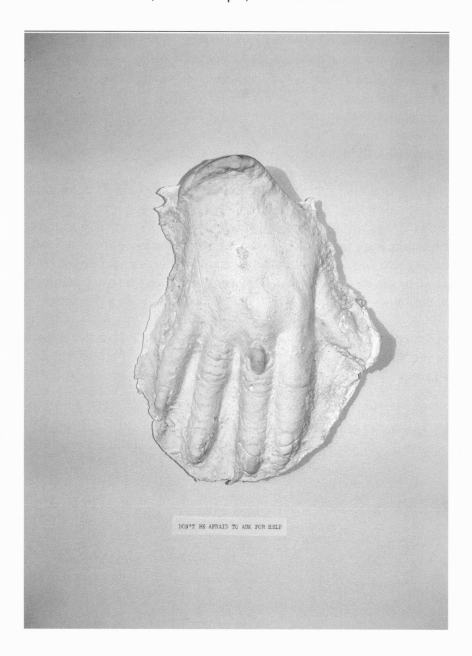

'The most natural thing'

Even when I had my kids I didn't really stop the drugs.

My children weren't affected by the drugs; they weren't born addicted, although one of them died inside of me. My housing advisor said to me, "it's good luck you lost the baby otherwise you would have lost this flat".

I gave birth at home when my youngest daughter was born and I haemorrhaged – my brother came round and said it looked like someone had slaughtered a pig in the house. Drugs had made me so weak that I nearly died doing the most natural thing.

All my kids have been taken off me. Their grandparents got a residency order for the girls. They used to stay with them at weekends while I went to Leicester. One weekend while I was away, my ex and his dad came and messed my house up to prove to the authorities that I was an unfit mother. Consequently the social workers told me I couldn't have the kids. I'll get them back, though. When they are sixteen they can do whatever they want; I know they want to live with me. My eldest daughter already spends as much time as she can with me.

My son was adopted while I was in prison. I was off the heroin for a while and just having crack now and again. But someone reported me to the social workers and one night while I was breastfeeding my son, they broke in with the police and took him from me. I don't really remember much about that time because it screwed me up so much. I don't know where he is now. I've got a photo of him though.

... he was so beautiful.

-

'You're my friend'

You're my Friend

See in the past or present we all need

We lose and with we have found

Me ; I lost it all in one hand

See there He was the mirror I seeked for.

My love; He made my seeing eyes feel whole

Separate from all senses

I dropped my heart locked so far in my rolling head

Eighty minute love affair that were

It should stay if you have to lose your way

Not what hell I should have lived half my sorry life.

He loved me; He would want me with him more and more

Then He never left my side

In the beginning I could keep up with His demanding ways,

Not for long

Pain is that love

The thing He had me do just to get deeper within me,

He had no time for pain

As they would whisper "He made you all warm and well"

SHIT

See not that bad, you'll be better shortly

We can all be weak and

I sit here today as your friend

He is oh so not good

Who said better than sex? See get a new one

He is not your love, your friend

in that more pain no one should test

It just goes on till you give up

And let him within and wrap his hot fiery arms around me to cut out
the cold chills

But His love is short-lived

In one hand he gives so much

And within a breeze He's ripped that blanket away.

So I stand here today as your friend

Do not be drawn in by his intrigue, all his stupid paraphernalia

Oh yes He swears he will keep you safe

All I say as your friend that He is bad and no good shall come from him

Just think of the worst pain you have had and multiply by more than your mind can hold and you might be close!

It's hot and if the shit's bad within a split sec you're cold, wet.

His silver nail showing hisself.

Sweating wet and cold, legs like a two year old; pain within growing.

He just teases and tempts you; in the same hand He has the power to snap you

Before no time you don't see you.

Who is me? I found love and lost the love for I.

So if something or someone has done you wrong, I could not ever put it on them.

So I say from my heart "why would you have it done to you or me?" I did.

We all have no way in the world to let one more soul see His hand.

We all have flames so we don't want His fire.

Keep your heart pure

I am here on the page and she is in the warmth of the sun

If you look real close within the spectrum you just might see a glimpse of "I am your friend"

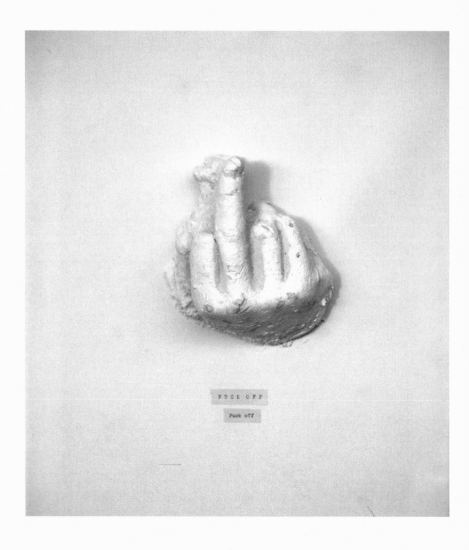

'Schoolgirl crush'

I didn't take drugs when I was little.

I used to look after my little brother while my mum got off her face. I wanted to go to school and learn but sometimes it was impossible. I had to keep an eye on mum and cook for us all. I was just a normal kid though; having fun with my friends, playing in the park, listening to music.

Then when I was about thirteen my mum gave my brother and I a little tube while she and her friends were all smoking. That's how I got hooked. Curiosity got me; I saw my parents having fun when they were off their head and I thought it looked great. And it became habit just like that. I was addicted dead quickly- it only took about four weeks. My mum would even score for me sometimes.

Whenever my brother and I got nice things, such as presents, they got sold for the drugs. I pinched things from shops to sell too.

To pay for my addiction I started working the streets, sleeping with men for money. Some of them really like schoolgirls. If I was wearing school uniform, I always got loads of work.

The first time I did it I was so nervous that I was shaking. You get used to it though; it's just a job in the end. I used to enjoy getting ready for work, putting on all of my make-up and looking like I was okay. I was always sober – some girls were always pissed but I used to think, you wouldn't go to work drunk if you worked in a bank, would you? I think my regulars approved; I was able to work without almost passing out. Not all working girls are on drugs though. When I was at my worst I was spending £150 to £200 a day on drugs, on anything I could get my hands on; speed, crack, weed, heroin. I wouldn't sleep for two or three days. I would get one night's sleep and then be back out there earning my money.

I had punters all day and night.

'Little but white'

Where fore I paint my way

The life hangs on the wall

We get to paint in the pieces

Where do we all fit?

The brush is my 'to be oh so free'

Long shiny nails, angelic smile

Full lash, powdered skin

Blood lip draining all the love from all the other paintings

Hanging on the oh so many walls

See in my painting there's free love

Quick flash of light

I'm flying dressed all in little but white

'A little snippet '

I left home at the age of 12 and started sleeping rough-and when I say rough I mean in the worst places you can think of.

I have slept on benches, in parks and public toilets. I regularly slept in the men's toilets at bus stations. I reckoned that if a pervert was looking for a girl he wouldn't look in the men's toilets would he? The staff there were lovely and used to even wash my clothes out for me. I used to wash myself and keep clean that way.

It was warm and safe...

' My mum's a prostitute and my dad's a pimp.'

My mum is a prostitute and my dad is a pimp.

He's got 18 kids with different women but only one son, so obviously most of the girls are prostitutes. I took my younger sister out of it, but I went through everything with my sister and my mum. I've really seen everything.

I've seen my mum being raped. I've had stages where my dad has brought people back into the house for her, or my sisters.

I got raped when I was 5 years old and I basically went ballistic at men.

My dad tortured women. That's what I call it, even to this day. I couldn't do prostitution and so I chose drugs because I knew I could handle that.

I was 9 and I was stealing some of his skunk and my dad caught me. Asked me if I had the money for it. I didn't. So he gave me an ounce of his stuff to drop off at a house and I did it and he gave me the weed. My friends thought it was great. Little by little he drew me in.

Someone rang me and asked me to bring them an ounce and I said no. My dad dragged me out and told me to go and I said no. So my dad sexually assaulted me in the front room to prove that he was the man. He made me give him a blowjob. That's how he proved his point.

My sisters got into it because they were living with mom and then they began to think oh it'll be better with dad, and it was better, for a couple of weeks. Then he got them into it.

Now most of us have just left and gone, even moved out of the county altogether.

I don't see all of them. I'm still really protective over my baby sister even though she's 22.

I can associate with men. I can deal with men. But when it comes down to it all I see is violence. I see them as my dad.

I still live in the same house as my dad. I live there but I'm not there. It's just really that I'm a lodger.

You go in my bedroom and you'd actually think it was a prison cell. Once I'm in that room I'm in that room.

When I've had conversations with my mum about why she's a prostitute we don't see eye to eye.

They met when she was 14 and she came from a very broken, very strict home. He was married. At 19 she had me. Then my younger sister and to her she was then trapped. At least that's how she sees it. I see it as weak.

My dad is a serial cheater simple. If he fancies it he's going to go and do it.

She had this degree of freedom, more than she'd ever had at home. She kept doing the things she was doing to provide him with things.

I left home when I was 9 and went to live with my big sister. I then went to live with my grandma but then my granddad got really ill and I had to go home.

One day I came back from basketball and walked in the house and my dad was beating my mum so I grabbed my sister, didn't even pack a bag, and we left to my grandmas.

The only woman he can't stand up to is my grandma.

I used to go to the forest park with my mates and then one time I come out and my mum's on the forest road in a leather dress. I was like "what are you doing?" she said she was going to the shops and I asked "what like that?" then a car pulled up and she got into it in front of me and all my mates.

It got to the point where if I didn't do something things were going to happen to my mum and obviously I had to care for my younger sister and me.

I've never seen a girl play football like my sister used to. I used to get her into after school things to keep her out of it. Then for that time I knew she was safe. She didn't know what I was doing, but she was safe.

I always have been her mum. Because if I'm not there who will be.

My biggest fear is that she'll end up in that situation where she thinks it's normal. And it's not normal to get battered round the head because the dinner isn't hot enough.

Then I got with my partner and he said we should start skimming. I had 3 jobs and I was doing all this and worrying about me, my partner and my younger sister, some nights I only had an hour and a half sleep.

My grandma doesn't know.

Outside the house we are all happy families. If you say something out of line you'll get it when you get back. My grandma thinks he's this lovely man who takes care of my mum. He's like a fucking monster. Simple. That's what he feeds off. If he doesn't get it he stomps and stamps until he gets it.

At 6 years old I was asking my dad if he was my dad? I already knew what my parents did. I was having a conversation with my friend about our parents' jobs and I said "my mums a prostitute and my dads a pimp." She then told her parents and they told my dad.

You teach a kid from a very young age that an apple is an orange then they're going to grow up thinking that it's an orange. I thought it was normal.

One time my mum had a punter upstairs and I was bouncing about downstairs hyper. The punter heard and wanted to know what was going on so my dad came down, saw my mums black stiletto lying about and threw it at me. I think he meant it to go behind my head but because I was jumping about it hit me in the eye. They asked me about it at school and I said my dad hit me in the eye with a shoe. You don't think about it when you're a kid. They got social services on the phone about me from a very young age.

I think the only good thing that came out from my mum and my dad was my sister. I don't think I could have coped without her. When I went to prison I was worrying about my sister. She was only 14 when I got sentenced to 5 years. Thinking about getting back to her was what made me keep my head down. I got out in 3 years.

My sister didn't cope when I went to prison. She became a very heavy drinker. Suddenly she had to see everything that I'd kept her from.

When I was 18 I was with a very abusive partner who I knew was cheating on me. I was pregnant and he kicked me from the top of the stairs to the bottom and I lost my daughter. That sent me off the rails and was how I ended up in prison. I did something bad and I knew I was going to get caught. But I feel really guilty because it was selfish of me not to think of my sister. I went to prison for my own selfish reasons.

I was hurt and I suffered and that was the only way I could get it out. I made them suffer. If you ask anyone my age round here they'd say I was fucking psychotic. But I'm not, I can channel it now, but when I was a kid I didn't care.

One time my sister threw me a surprise party and some guy showed up that my sister had issues with. I was upstairs and someone told me that he pinned her against a wall. I went psycho and grabbed a knife. My friends tackled me to the floor and hid my knives in the washing machine. The next morning what did I do. I turned the washing machine on.

I used to have problems. People are a puzzle, you've got all these little bits and you've got to slot them altogether. I'm still trying to work mine out and make it fit.

A big part of the problem is that my mum won't leave my dad. I don't understand her. I don't think there's anything that she wouldn't put up with for him. He's stripped everything away from her. You watch them destroy each other and there's nothing you can do. Either you break the cycle or you close ranks.

4 years old and you're hitting your mum over the head with a crow bar because she picked up your baby sister to protect her. That's not normal.

Once I ended up losing my head over this one bouncer who looked like my dad. I got this big fucking rage in my head and I just wanted to tear his head off.

I know that one day I'll have a breakdown and I wont be able to cope.

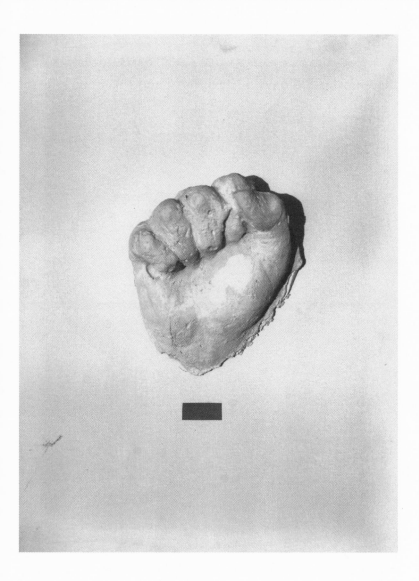

'Red hot'

I started selling weed, was a drug-dealer then went into prostitution.

I was abused by my uncle and left home at 9. I worked as a cashier for Tesco it was "crap". I knew how to manipulate men- 'pussy in their face.' I used what I knew. I'm tidy; I never leave condoms and treat my punters nicely. I have 3 children and can build computers. I've now been banned from the red-light district; usually this drives girls into crack dens.

I don't work the streets so much anymore. I have my regulars and usually they come to my flat. Some of them have been coming for years and I have a great deal of trust in most of them, but just occasionally I have to protect myself. On one occasion I had gone to a new blokes flat, and when I was getting myself ready for him he appeared with a pair of scissors at my vaginal area and wanted to cut my pubic hair!

I punched him in the throat and escaped pretty sharpish!

'To lie about love'

The same time every day

I kiss the kids goodbye and go on my way.

A bed, a street, a lonely bar, or sometimes in a stranger's car.

To lie about love,

To wipe my face of greasy skin and clammy chest.

To scuff my shoes and tear my skin.

I will do all this to bring the money in.

For you my Darling child.

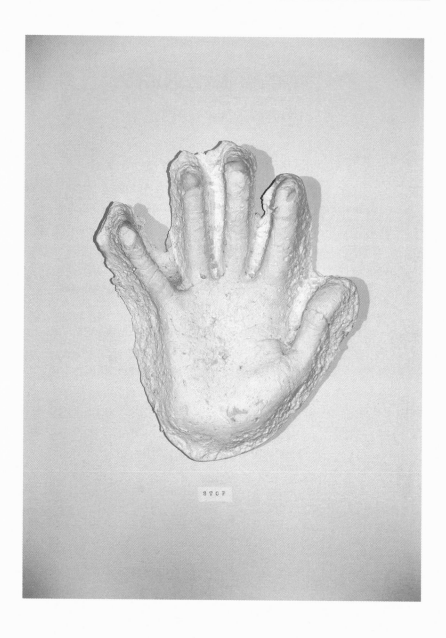

Poem from a Working Woman

I used to work all night,

I used to work all day,

And I practically gave my body away

I used to hate myself for the life I led,

As all day long men were in my bed

But now that's all changed,

And I've grown up a lot and never again,

Will I pretend to be something I am not

"Dirty Bitch", "Clap Trap", "Whore", "Slapper", "Slag",

"Mary", "Hooker", "Streetwalker", "Prostitute", "Ho", "Tom", "Loose", "Goose", "Skettle".

That's what some of the "gentlemen" out there call us working girls. They treat you like shit and wouldn't even piss on you if you were on fire. I've been spat at, had milk bottles thrown at me, I've had full coke cans chucked at my head. These "gentlemen" make disrespectful comments like, "go suck out your mother". I've lost count of the number of times I've had my hair pulled or been slapped. A punter even broke my sternum (my breast bone) because I wouldn't give him oral sex without a condom. We don't tend to have pimps to look after us round here so we all look out for each other.

It doesn't keep us safe all the time.

'Stay out of the game'

Don't waste your life

I try not to act funny when I hear my friends are dying,

Is it the crack cocaine that smashes up their brain?

Or the heroin that sends them insane?

I'm not lying they say the drinks just the same,

I come out the game; people are looking at me like I'm not the same,

I've got money in my pocket, money on my mind,

I don't want to go back to the same silly game,

I know everybody's name,

It's like I'm crying for the living and the dying,

Don't waste your life don't waste your life

STAY OUT OF THE GAME!!!

By A.S

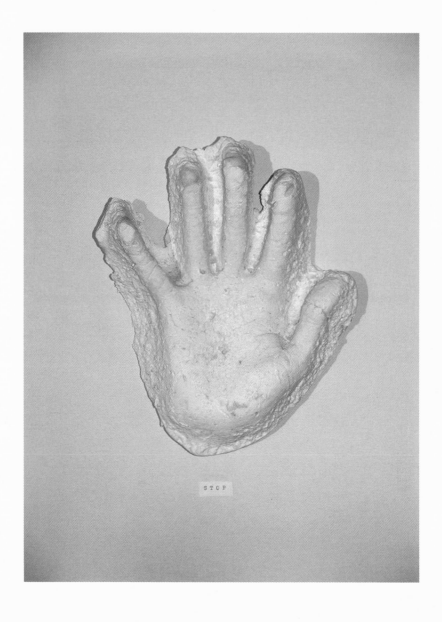

'Him'

We're going back about 12-13 years ago and it all started on a night out on the town with the lads.

I was with three friends at the time; three guys. As we were walking up I got approached by a girl, she said "I've had a fight with my boyfriend", and asked to borrow a couple of pounds to get the bus home.

It turned out it was an old girlfriend from school. I got talking to her and gave her a tenner and my phone number. A couple of days later she gets in touch and starts telling me her story.

She left school at 15 and got straight into drugs. Had a couple of offences and the courts got to her and then eventually she got involved in prostitution. She told me she was sofa surfing and she ended up living at mine.

At first she was doing fine physically she looked a lot better. And she said she was coming off all the drugs. She asked for money and I did what I could. But then it got worse and she started stealing things and disappearing. But by this time we were in a relationship.

I knew nothing about the drugs and so I didn't understand all the things she was doing.

I got so frustrated that in a stupid moment I thought if I can't beat you I'll join you. So I had a little smoke of a crack pipe. A few days later we were having a drive and I started getting a watery mouth and I said to her do you fancy some more of that stuff? And that was it. I had quite a lot of money and so it was easy to get drugs. Very easy.

By this point I was accepting of what she was doing, the prostitution and all that, and so I started watching her back. You're skulking in and out of alleys watching her and taking number plates of cars she gets into and waiting for her to get dropped off again.

It's all about the girl surviving you see.

I started offending myself to get more money. I've been in prison a couple of times.

By this point the relationship is chaotic and there's times when I barely see her. I had a little plan where we put an escort add in the paper instead. She's making more money, I can drive her there, and it's better. But the more money means that we're smoking more drugs.

Eventually the escort thing crumbled. The police seized the car and we spent all the money on drugs.

A couple of times we did a show for punters. No touching, they just wanted to watch.

From doing the drugs I begin to know more people on the drug scene. I get girls asking me to watch their backs. I set up lot of little escort lines but they never last long.

One time this drug dealer asked me to go get him some drugs. I got stopped on the way back. There was 2kg of cocaine and 6lb of ganja in that suitcase. When I stood up in court and they only announced the charges of 6lb ganja, not the cocaine I was amazed. I spent 2 months in a Jamaican prison. Bread and water for breakfast. 10x10 cell with 10guys and 5 beds.

Once I was back in England I was straight back onto it.

I've been in a few relationships with girls on the beat. You have no idea where they're going to go or whether they're going to come back you spend all your time worrying.

I've told myself now, no more girls until I'm off drugs.

Last week, an old working girlfriend turned up at my house out of the blue asking to stay. She stayed a couple of days and then went out to work and I haven't seen her since.

I never say no to girls asking to stay. I cant see a friend on the street with no where to go.

Silent killer :

One time she was staying with me and I was dealing drugs to feed my own habit. A guy came round and he had a brand new nokia N95. I swapped this phone for drugs. She put sleeping pills in my drink that night and when I woke up the she and the phone were missing, I didn't see her again for 6 months. Until she came back asking to stay again.

M:

At Christmas, we are out shoplifting, getting perfumes etc. later in afternoon we come back to the flat. While I go to get fish and chips, M takes the perfumes and disappears.

I've had so many messy relationships. But also love.

'Red light'

Red light

I am a woman who walks the area of the red light,

Used by the needy and lonely men by day or night,

The law want it stopped, try as they might to get this trade out of sight!

Some girls are true to form, some like to con!

But the street life will go on.

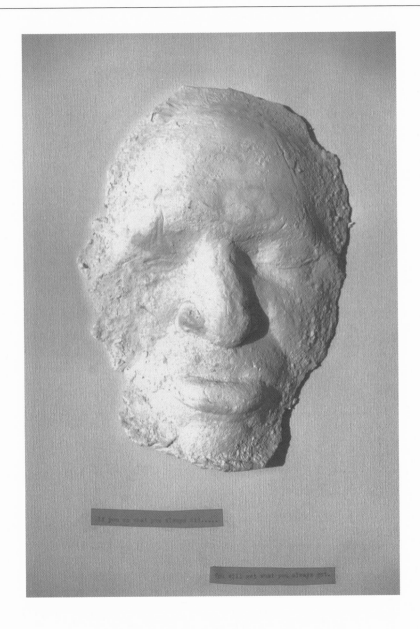

'Junkie's Psalm'

The Junkie's psalm

King heroin is my shepherd,

I shall always be in want,

He makes me lie down in the gutters,

He leads me beside troubled waters,

He destroys my soul,

He leads me in the paths of wickedness,

For the effort's sake,

Yes, I shall walk through the valley of poverty,

And fear all evil, for you, heroin are with me,

Your needle and capsule try to comfort me,

They stripped the table of groceries,

In the presence of my family,

You rob my head of reason,

My cups of sorrows runs over,

Surely heroin addiction shall stalk me,

All the days of my life,

And I will dwell in the house of the dammed forever.

(Adapted from a poem written by a twenty-year-old heroin addict based on Psalm 23. She left it typed on a card in a telephone booth).

'Two white and a dark'

Two White and a Dark

Arise anytime night or day

Two white and a dark are the words I say

A deadly rattle is on its way

I start to swear and sometimes pray

Two white and a dark are the words I say

Got to go out make a raze any damn way

Two white and a dark are the words I say

Day after day.

Six months the judge did say

and on that beautiful freedom day damn it

Two white and a dark are the words I say Depressed frowned upon and ill every day

Two white and a dark I'm trying hard not to say

The years roll by, skeleton frame old and grey

Two white and a dark God help me please not to say

Looked out my window the other day watch my kids play

Two white and a dark I heard them say

'Kidnapped'

I was picked up on the beat by a foreign looking guy, he said he wanted to do business.

The punter pulled up to the kerb in a taxi, I asked him if he wanted business he said yes we agreed a price and I agreed to go with him to his home address. During the taxi ride the punter was chatting away and telling me how he had just brought a derelict pub and that's where we were going, I wasn't too bothered I just wanted to get the £60.00 he had promised me and then go and score.

We arrived at this derelict building and once inside, I told him that I wasn't going to do anything with him until I got my money—he assured me that he was going to give me my money but wanted to relax with a drink first. He told me that the drink was stored in the cellar and I believed him and followed him down into the cold, damp, dark cellar. The lights weren't on, I couldn't see anything but I was aware that he had locked the door and I was on my own. I don't know how long I was down there for, hours? I was screaming and making up noise trying to get someone's attention—no one came. After what seemed like 3 or 4 hours, I heard the door open and the punter came down the stairs and forced me to perform oral sex on him after the act he went out again locking the door behind him. This was repeated over the 4 days that I was kept imprisoned, he would come down stairs subject me to sexual abuse and leave me locked up.

During the days of being kept captive he began to take me upstairs to the bedroom, where he subjected me to horrific rapes. I was in fear for my life, I didn't know if he was going to have let me go, or just kill me when he had finished with me. I began to talk to him, I told him about my daughter and that I had to get home to look after her, he wanted me to stay with him it's as if he thought we were in a relationship.

As the days progressed, the punter began to let down his guard and he would leave me in the room whilst he used the bathroom. On one such occasion I was able to use his mobile phone and dial 999- he came in whilst I was on the phone to the police and he grabbed the phone and ended the call. He was shouting at me calling me a stupid bitch and now I was in trouble, a short time later the phone rang and this really made him angry. He dragged me down the stairs and pushed me out the door to a waiting taxi, I screamed in the taxi and told him that I had been raped and was being held against my will. The punter punched me in my face, got out of the cab and ran off. I tried to explain to the taxi driver what had happened but he was only concerned about who was going to pay the fare, when I said that I didn't have any money he pulled over and made me get out. I was stranded.

I phoned the police who was aware of me because my partner had reported me missing, the police picked me up and took me home. During my journey home I was asked by the police if I knew exactly where I had been taken—I didn't have a clue!

The police offered me little sympathy and gave me a lecture, something like; at the end of the day you know that your job is risky, you are suppose to take notice of where you are, so when you start remembering give us a call.

I didn't call them back.

'Pain of the Trap'

Pain

No ones pain is filtered to that bubble

Within it you can't see clear

And hear not so much

Sounds fun-No!

Within the snake satisfied your vein

He fights his way around your bones

To have him just not satisfied

Crack, snap, pop goes your head

Time to get scared, the chills are in

O so within your body, soul and mind

Who in their right mind would let their soul or mind be violated as my body?

I don't care that much for him inside me

You just don't see how erratic you become.

Trap

Falling into the trap

The taste you miss

Greed takes away the taste

It's been that long I seem to have forgot 'BASH'

All just go to bashing

See, hear all your users

Let's stand apart from all that greed—rebel

Who misses the real itch?

No nor I!

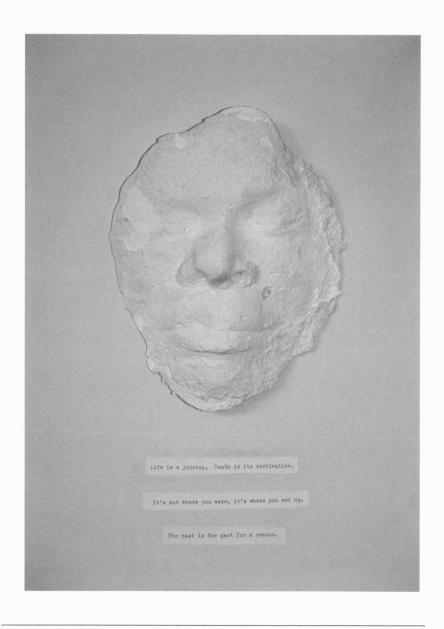

'Love is only a little word'

My Childhood was absolutely brilliant.

I had a fantastic family, wonderful Mum and Dad . . . Yea I think my childhood was like what normal children do, I had fun, went to a Catholic school in Nottingham, went to church on a Sunday.

Dad was in the building trade, mum had 3-5 jobs cleaning to give us a good upbringing. There was so much love in the home, yea fights too but just what normal families do. As I got to my teens I had lots of support educationally yet as I reached around 15/16 I began to test things,

I was very curious. I had a friend who was very close to me called Tina, we would go out, you know nightclubs, youthclubs. We had good times, my parents always said come back at 10. so, you know, we came back at 11. Got a little telling off, stuff like that.

It was difficult, you know having not much money, I had hand-me-down clothes and shoes. But we didn't really care, the love in the house was more than enough for us.

Then I fell in love at 16, he became my daughter's father. He was a black guy and at that time, there was a bit of prejudice, my family wasn't happy with the relationship. He was 2 or 3 years older. I left school at the age of 16, while I was still going out with him and the love just grew and grew.

I had a job in Woolworths, wasn't happy with that so got a job as a window dresser. First I worked on the floor, I had a great relationship with the manager and when a post came out for a junior window dresser I got it. I worked my way from junior to senior window dresser and did that for a few years.

Things had become difficult at home as I hadn't yet ended the relationship, so my dad asked me to leave the family unit, more than not because of his race. So I left the house and got a flat on Derby Road with my friend Tina. We shared the rent, and to pay for that I got a second job in a bar. I worked all day, at night time too. I also got a job in a factory, so I had 3 jobs to help pay rent, buy food and a source of survival, a means of independence.

At that time Tina then didn't want to stay in the flat, so she left, leaving me with all the bills. I was still in my relationship; he worked at a major firm at the time. But I was struggling, and struggling to try and make ends meet.

I had a friend in prostitution that was working and I went to visit her, I had known her from growing up. She was close to me and I think no matter what your friends do, you don't shy away from it. I went to her one night and asked her to teach me how to be a prostitute, she refused, at first. I told her; "even if you help or not, I'm still going to do it".

I got ready and went where I knew the beat was. It was a hard decision. I think at the time I didn't feel I was being coerced by my partner, you know because I was young.

It was hard for me, a bit devastating. I was scared, panicking but I will always remember when I went down there.

Back at that time the price for a hand relief was £5. I was 19, it was the early 1970's.

I didn't know what I felt at the time. All I knew I was so determined to not go back to my family and ask for help, I am very proud. And that's how I began working. From that day I went down there, I never stopped.

At the time I wasn't too worried of the dangers, I had my friends watching my back. At that time the prostitution community were together out there, they looked after each other, not even 95%, I mean 100%.At that time If I went in a car and no one saw me get in, I would write down using chalk the number plate on the pavement so that they knew I had gone off with a punter.

I wasn't weary, I had more than my eyes out there looking over me, and we were there for each other.

I carried the other jobs on for a bit, but it was a lot to do. I was tired, I was at the factory from 4:30am, would come home and get ready, go to the window dressing job, then onto the bar job then onto the street. I got No sleep. I worked the streets for a while, and then it got to the stage where I wanted not to stop but not to work outside. I was weary of my family seeing me, even a friend of a friend. I had to be so alert out there. I didn't just think about me. I didn't want my family to be affected.

My life was separate, I worked but never bought it home, not where I lived and slept. I was still with my boyfriend, he knew. I loved him.

The relationship carried on for 29 years. a few years after it was over I found out he had a woman and children.

I had fallen in love. It was too hard to walk away, but I wish I had had the strength to. My heart was too in it, it made me bitter, angry that he hadn't told me the truth. Then he soon had other women, he wasn't just sleeping with me; and I was still working, still carrying on with the relationship.

I carried on with this for years but then the domestic violence started. The power trip; "you're not going out". It didn't work, if you tell me not do something I will do it.

I went out and he would be there with another woman in the nightclub. Somehow despite it all I would end up giving him £100, £200.

He'd say he loved me, and I carried on and carried on and carried on. It is why I always say to anyone who asks, that though love is only a little word, only 4 letters, but it can become very powerful, it can overtake your life. It took mine.

I moved from the streets to saunas. At that time I could easily get in a sauna as I wasn't using drugs. Drug using at that time was rare, it was not an issue at all. We had Alcohol now and again, but only when we weren't working, and speed just because we worked long hours it was to carry us through the day.

We didn't take it to lose ourselves, we were paid for our body; it was a job. The money does get addictive though, like a drug. I never valued the money as such as I wouldn't have given it away so easily.

I went to work in Germany for a few weeks when I was about 28, my daughter was taken care of by my Mum for a fortnight.

My Mum didn't know what I was up to. I used to work all over; London, Doncaster, Leicester, Bournemouth. I have been everywhere.

My friend went to London, came back all bubbly and said she had met an agency that wanted to take us to Germany. I said "yeh sounds good". How wrong I was.

We were met by two massive guys in Keele, Germany. They took us to the club where we were going to work. They told us to give them our passports, I had no choice, they grabbed me and told us no passport, no work. They had set my alarm bells ringing, so I stole and made a copy of the office key.

We had rooms above the club upstairs where we lived. There were also rooms for paying customers. There were loads of English, German and American punters in Keele. You had to sell them a bottle of Champagne first, about a £100. You got £25, the club got £75, then they got a percentage out of what you earnt upstairs, which was pittance.

One night at 2'oclock in the morning, I said to my friend pack your bags, stole back our passports and ran for it to the train station to Hamburg and ended up in a proper club in Tria, I danced there, earning money on my dancing and the other things too.

When we came back I couldn't get in the saunas back in Nottingham as they were all full.

My daughter was young, when she went to school I would work, when she was back I wouldn't. The vice caught me, the newspaper published my name for getting nicked from prostitution and my family all had to read it. I will always remember that.

I had lived two lives, they had no idea I was working. My dad used to banter with me how I never came back to ask for money or help, I always told him I was okay. When he read it, he disowned me, told me my Surname wasn't ********** anymore. That he didn't have a daughter anymore.

I respected him for that, how he felt. My partner was still around.

In my early 30's I tried crack cocaine. I had worked all that time not really touching drugs, I knew people used it but I had never really felt like doing it. Curioristy killed the cat. I was addicted for 8 years.

Finally back working in the Sauna, for 12 hours a day I presented myself well to the punters. I earnt 3-4-5-600 pounds a day. I spent all of it on crack. Getting hooked was almost an accident, I had just wanted to try it. I enjoyed it, just like you do smoking cigarettes. I knew it had got to the point where I was tired of my life. So I ended it in the saunas, I still had certain regulars but Iturned to shoplifting, stealing cheque books, nicking cards, whatever got me money.

I have had a couple of bad punters, one was when Jack the Ripper was around. The media thought he was coming to the Midlands. The police came round and knocked on my door and other working girls, told us to be careful about punters, especially if there were tools in the back of the car. He used to drive round with claw hammers, stuff like that. But you know, if your punter is in the building trade, he will have tools in the back, so anyone could've been Jack the Ripper.

It was a rainy night just after midnight, I went out and I didn't follow my instincts. I got in this car and I didn't feel right, even talking to him wasn't right. But I got in it, it was cold, I wanted to get home. We reached Canning Circus and something said to me 'you're gonna die'.

I had a feeling, something bad, and I mean bad. I told him to take a right and go down Ilkeston Road, not Derby Road. He just swung his hand and thumped me, my whole jaw was thrown sideways.

I thought "ohh shit, my daughters at home and he is going to kill me, he's going to kill me." All I could see in my head was my daughter. He kept beating me, whilst driving fast, each time I went for the wheel or tried to talk, he wacked me again, I was covered in blood and bruises everywhere. My heart stopped when I looked back between the seats and saw a dustsheet covering things. My jaw had been near enough broken, my nose was in bits. I saw the island at the bottom of the road, and I told myself I'm turning this car. I don't care how much he whacks me. All I thought of was my daughter, I grabbed the wheel and the car flipped. I was a time for desperate measures, I had kept trying to swerve the car down Derby Road, praying I would hit something and stop, run away. I went into pilot mode. Being half upside down, I could hear sounds from him, I thought "you bastard". I smashed the window with my feet, he wanted help, but I knew he wasn't going to die . . . (he deserved to though) . . . so I got out and I just ran.

Yes it shook me up; but you know just patch yourself up, put some makeup on and you'll be okay.

I had built up quite a good bunch of regulars, So after that I didn't really having to go out again to meet strangers.

We all used to be strong females but to fight a man, you will never be strong enough. It was a façade of strength, many men respected it, but some didn't.

My boyfriend knew, but he was too busy collecting money off everyone else. He knew I would be out of action for a while, whilst my body healed.

He had a few other working girls. He was a charmer.its not that I blame him, I didn't blame him at the time, I just thought I would go with the flow. But as I got older I began to stand up for myself more, challenge him. I wanted to stop the drugs, he didn't at the time. I sat down, and reflected, I wanted to save myself so I could take care of my daughter, gain that love back, because when she became teenager things began to click in her head about what I was doing.

She knew about the drugs though but not the prostitution. That began a time where I really had to think about what I was doing and how. I would always get to 3 weeks of being clean, then I would be back on the crack. I hated myself for it. One Sunday I came in after a bender and my daughter just looked at me, said to me "don't say a word Mum, you always say never again". She left home for a bit, she was 14. I was taking a lot, I wouldn't just buy one rock, I would buy ounces.

The drugs and the saunas were separate, you didn't see the drug dealers like you today. The boyfriends nearly all do it today. Now it's all about the drugs. Someone said to me other day that when you get through your recovery, you know you have won when you can't remember. You've moved on.

When my daughter walked out I was devastated. but even then I knew it was the best thing for her to do. It gave me the biggest shake up of my life. That day was dark, I was ready to take my life. When she'd gone I looked at myself. Got a bottle of vodka, a collection of pills. I knew what I was doing. I cut the telephone lines. It wasn't a cry for help, I just couldn't cope anymore. Something in me, in the room, just something, told me to look in the mirror in front of me and I hated what I saw. I saw me, first time, how I looked, tired, sunken, I looked 70. I hated it but I couldn't take my eyes off that image. I threw the bottle away, the pills away and I lay down and slept 2 whole days, nothing else. I got up, opened the curtains and looked outside and said, "I got to get through this this cant be the end of me." I remember for weeks being in that house, a known crack house, a place for smoking drugs, drug dealers. It was a battle, every time there was a knock, I would lie on the floor, if I answered it I would relapse. I told people I knew to not let me have any drugs, even drug dealers, they obliged.

I got through. I was feeling stronger and stronger, I needed to build bridges with my daughter. Sorry isn't a word to me, it is just a word she had heard me say it too much. I had to take my time with her and work through so she could see what I was doing was for real this time. I have rebuilt the bridges, she is no longer just my daughter but my best friend. Its been hard for her, I don't say sorry anymore as I cant undo what went on, but we work on it every day. I have two amazing grandchildren, Fiona and Thomas, I would not swap my life with anybody or for any amount of money. I love who I am now, the job I'm in too and I love my family.

Me and her dad had finished that relationship, It was not a clear cut finish but I stood my ground.

Now I can say, after all these years I realised he couldn't of loved me. I was a cash point card, that's how he thought of me, how he saw me. I still see him from time to time, I'm here and he is still there. I can smile because I know I am out, he is not. I do want the best for him, but he needs to want it for himself now.

Never say the word never, it doesn't exist. Having helped women who are still living my past, I think if they take one sentence from me, they can water that, treat it like a seed. It may take 2 years to grow but when I see them again I will give them the same sentence, and another sentence to build upon. It's about not closing the doors, not thinking your higher than them. Everyone is equal in this World. If you cut your wrist and I cut mine, its red blood.

Working girls should never stop believing, anyone can do anything they want to.

Through the jobs over the years one of my roles was being an outreach worker. I have met females and males, those who have offended, those who were homeless, those who used class A and those who have worked in prostitution. I didn't care if it was snowing, raining but I would get in that car and sit with them. Sit down on a grass verge, if that was the only time they felt it safe to talk cause their partner was standing meters away, watching. I would be there.

We cant put a time on anybody's life to change, we have no right to do that. Just work with them to the end of that journey, if they want you to. I don't know where I got this strength from, but no one could take that away from me now.

Just don't close the door. I had never had the chance to learn who I really was when I was a working girl. I Lived two lives, had two identities, prostitution tore my identity to shreds.

But what I did, it gave me the passion and strength to now support females and males in vulnerable situations. It was tough; but give me more tough things because it makes me a greater person, a stronger person.

Today, what I hear devastates me, most of the girls I see today, are on Class A, who are working in prostitution. Out there it hurts me, they're off their heads, not absorbing what you say. Their partners are like mine but they say their boyfriends love them. I say he is watching you, how much money your getting in.

What gives them the god dam right, how would they feel if it was their daughters on the streets. Girls aren't even together anymore, it's a lonely place out there for them now.

What do girls mean when they say they made a logical decision to enter prostitution? I thought I had made a logical decision to enter, but now I can honestly say, no one stopped me. Was it a logical decision? It's a major question mark in my life, it is likely I will never find the answer to.

Before my parents died they saw the turning point in me, I now have a proper smile, to wake up in the morning and see life as it is real. I will never stop helping working girls. Within our lives it's hard but as a drug I will carry on in my role as long as I can.

I believe it is never too late for anyone to change.

"If you cut your wrist,

and I cut mine,

it's still red blood."

POW Nottingham is a company limited by guarantee. It is registered in England and Wales with company number 06675269 and charity number 1129979. Its registered office is at 16 Independent Street, Radford, Nottingham NG7 3LN." The company is also a charity registered in England and Wales.

www.justgiving.com/pow-nottingham

Text POWS00 £5 to 70070 to donate to POW Nottingham Limited and make a difference today. JustTextGiving by Vodafone